classroom

SAVERS

classroom
LIFE
SAVERS

PETER
CLUTTERBUCK

Level One

Ashton Scholastic

SYDNEY AUCKLAND NEW YORK TORONTO LONDON

To the memory of Martin Carboon

The purchase of this book entitles the teacher to reproduce the black-line masters for classroom use.

Typeset by Veritage Press, West Gosford, NSW
Printed by Star Printery Pty Limited, Erskineville, NSW

10 9 8 7 6 5 4   9 / 8 0 1 2 3 / 9

Introduction

How many times during the school day do you wish there was something extra to give the class? Students often finish work early, have free time, need inspiring on rainy days, want a refreshing change to the usual homework tasks or need a 'brain warmer' at certain times of the day. *CLASSROOM LIFESAVERS* rescues you from all those moments.

Used as individual, group or whole class activities, *CLASSROOM LIFESAVERS* caters for the individual differences between children in a class. Level One gives activities for infants and covers the areas of word recognition, one-to-one correspondence, number recognition and observation.

Substitute teachers will wonder how they ever survived without *LIFESAVERS* — a wealth of fully reproducible activity sheets ready to use with children of any level.

Level One is set out in five sections, each with 18 work sheets.

The five sections are:
Word works
See and do
Number fun
Inside/outside
Puzzles

Level Two caters for the early primary years and **Level Three** for the later primary years. Word puzzles, general knowledge and vocabulary, teasers and logical puzzles, observation and memory, maths puzzles, and games for two or three are covered in these levels.

Most of the sheets require writing/colouring implements only, however the students should be encouraged to use concrete materials with the number sheets if they require them. A checklist and symbol key has been provided for your students to keep an easy record of the sheets they complete. You can also use this to show students particular sheets to complete — every sheet may not be suitable for every student. Photocopy the checklist and symbol key for each student.
Give students a folder in which to keep their completed sheets and have them glue the checklist to the inside cover.

CLASSROOM LIFESAVERS will make every minute in the classroom count. They will spark every student's idle moment.

My Checklist

Level One

Word works	Ww	1	2	3	4	5	6	7	8	9	10	11	12	13	14	15	16	17	18
See and do	Sd	1	2	3	4	5	6	7	8	9	10	11	12	13	14	15	16	17	18
Number fun	Nf	1	2	3	4	5	6	7	8	9	10	11	12	13	14	15	16	17	18
Inside/ Outside	Io	1	2	3	4	5	6	7	8	9	10	11	12	13	14	15	16	17	18
Puzzles	P	1	2	3	4	5	6	7	8	9	10	11	12	13	14	15	16	17	18

Name _____

Draw a line from the word to the picture.
Colour the picture.

bus bun bug 	tap top tip 
 mat man map	 cat can cap
bat bag bad 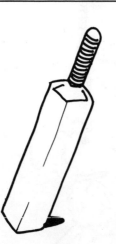	fin fig fir 

Name _____

Ww

Sheet 2

Make the word for the picture.

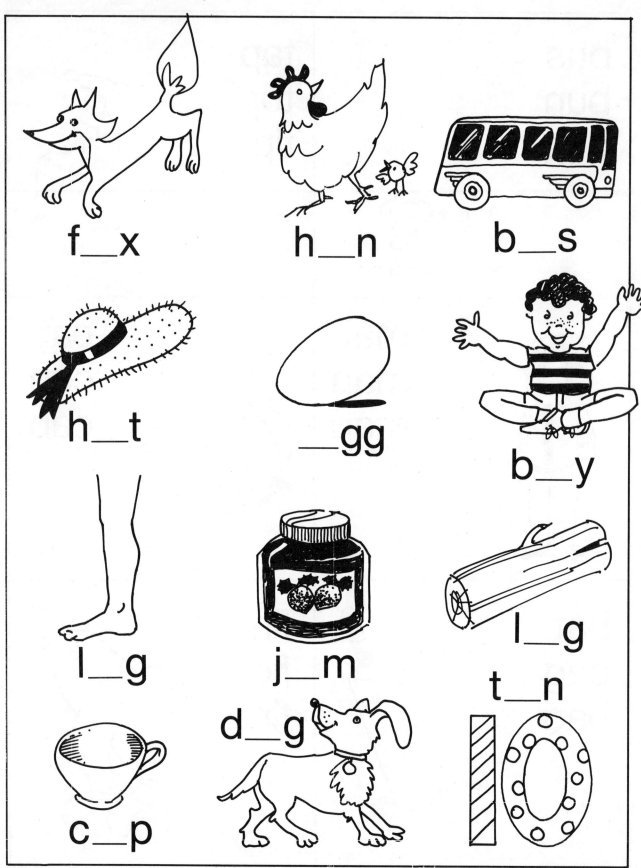

f__x

h__n

b__s

h__t

__gg

b__y

l__g

j__m

l__g

t__n

c__p

d__g

Name _____

Finish the word.

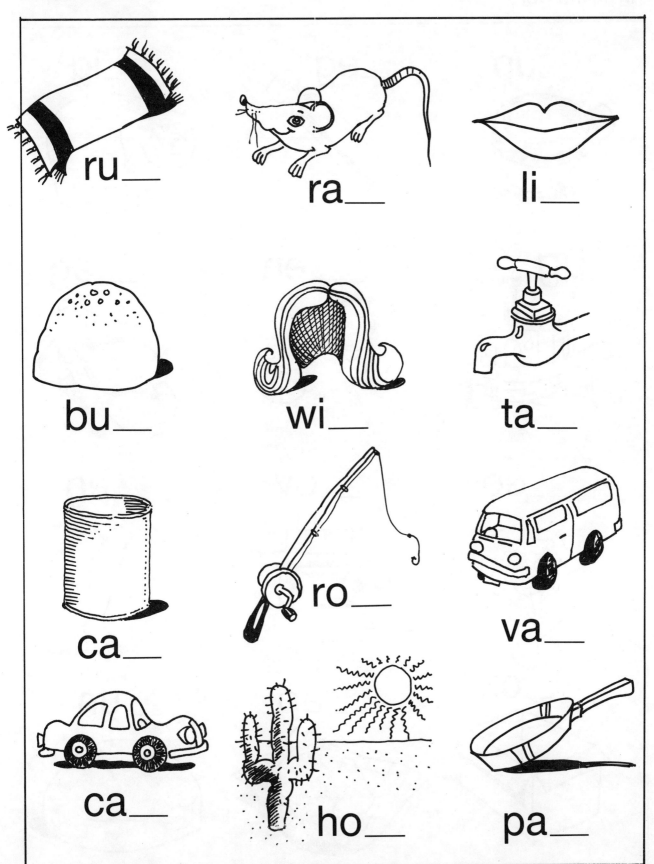

ru___

ra___

li___

bu___

wi___

ta___

ca___

ro___

va___

ca___

ho___

pa___

Name _____

Finish the word.

__up

__eg

__ig

__ug

__en

__ag

__eb

__oy

__eg

__ox

__ap

__un

Ww

Name _____

Unjumble the letters to make the word in the picture.
Write the word on the line.
Colour the picture.

puc

_____

naf

_____

apt

_____

gip

_____

art

_____

tyo

_____

gut

_____

upp

_____

Name _____

Add 'm' to each letter group and draw the picture.

__ap	__at	__an	__ug

Add 'b' to each letter group and draw the picture.

__ed	__us	__ox	__ell

Add 'f' to each letter group and draw the picture.

__ox	__ace	__an	__ence

Name _____

Ww

Sheet 7

Make the word for the picture. Colour the picture.

__at

__ox

__oy

b__n

s__n

d__g

__un

p__d

Change the order of the letters to make the word in the picture.

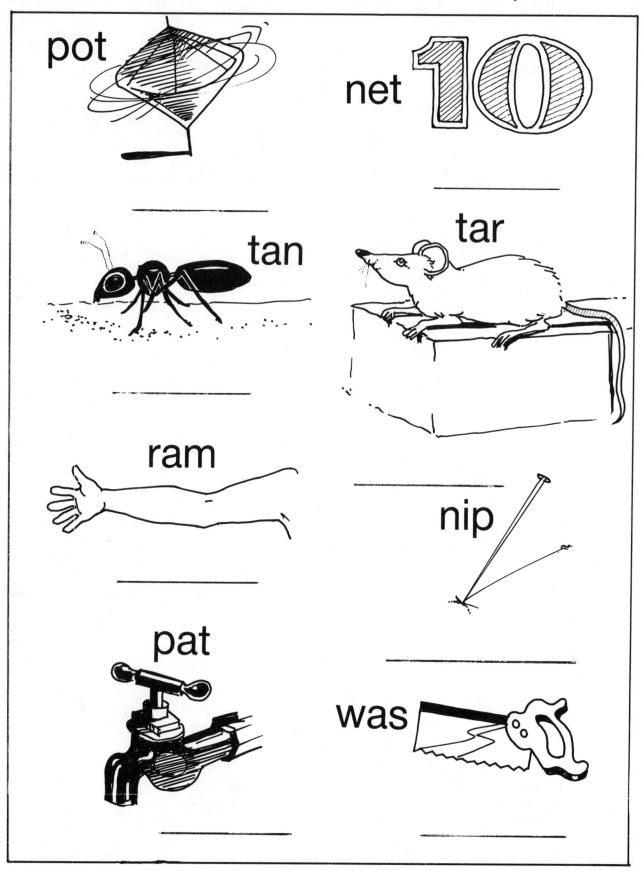

pot

net 10

tan

tar

ram

nip

pat

was

Name _____

Finish the word to match the picture.

__ate

__eat

pea__

win__

car__

__one

__top

__old

Name

Draw the missing pictures.

Ww

Sheet 10

son	sun	see	sea
meet	meat	flour	flower
sale	sail	bawl	ball
hare	hair	male	mail

Name _____

Draw a line from the word to the picture.
Colour the picture.

1

plate
gate
date
cage

2

stone
smoke
rose
nose

3

blue
glue
mule
true

4

brown
clown
fowl
crown

5

garden
carpet
farm
dark

6

wheel
wheat
ship
whale

Name _____

Colour the same colour, words in boxes that begin with the same sound.

shark	bring	shut
crab	ship	crow
break	crawl	brush

Draw a picture of two of these words.

Colour the same colour, words in the boxes that end with the same sound.

looked	bumpy	stacked
trying	picked	sweeping
happy	playing	pretty

Name _____

- Find a little word in the big word.
- Write the new word.
- Draw a picture of each little word.
- The first one has been done for you.

year	elephant	fowl
 ear _____	_____	_____

brain	seal	carrot
_____	_____	_____

Name _____

Word Sums

Join the word and the ending to make a bigger word.
Write the new word.

try+ing _____   sweep+ing _____

talk+ed _____   look+ed _____

crash+ing _____   creep+ing _____

brush+ed _____   splash+ed _____

Write in pairs, the words that have the same sound.
Draw a picture of two of these words.

frog	track	song	dog
shed	long	sack	said

_____ _____ _____ _____

_____ _____ _____ _____

Name

Write 'oo' or 'ee' in the space to make the word in the picture.

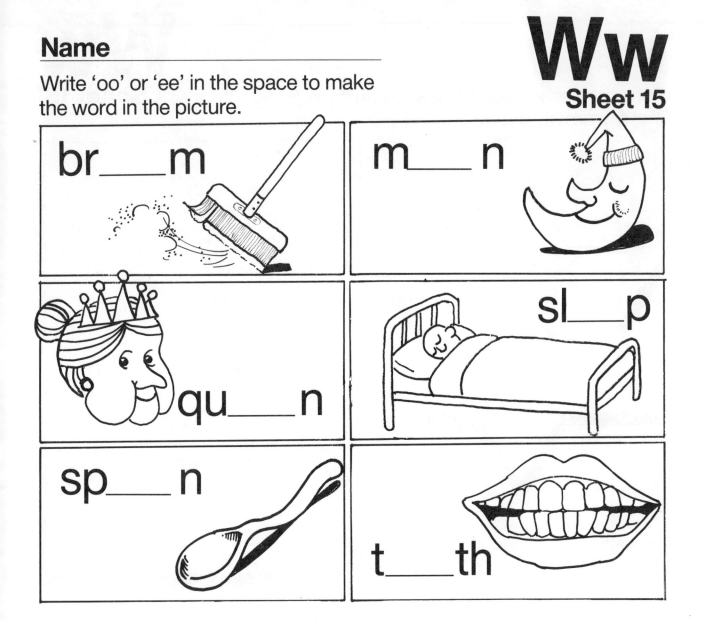

br___m

m___n

qu___n

sl___p

sp___n

t___th

Circle the word on the right that does not end with the same sound as the word on the left.

truck – black brick flock bring

mist – march twist list fist

edge – badge clock hedge ridge

clamp – stamp damp write lump

stiff – off stuff tramp cliff

Name

Put a circle around all those words in the box
that rhyme with the word in the star.

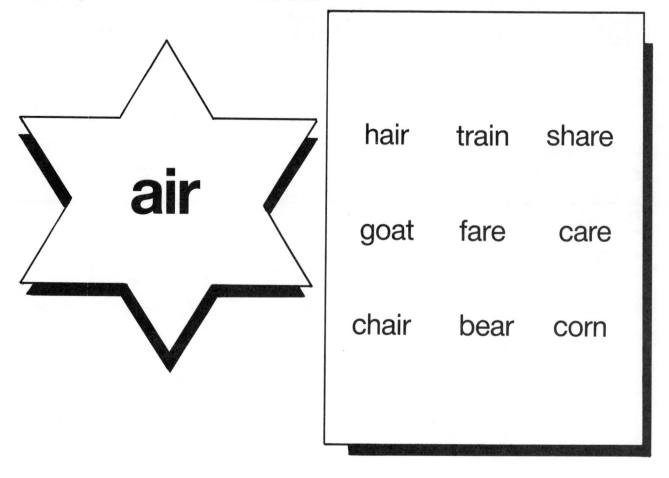

air

hair   train   share

goat   fare   care

chair   bear   corn

Here are four words joined together. Can you separate them?

trainrainstainchain

Name

Make as many words as you can by joining the letter group
in the centre to the other letter groups in the square.

di   cru   ell

all   fi

ed   sh   op

cra   ip

ut   spla   fla

Name _____

Change one letter in each word below to make
a word with 'ine' in it.
eg fire – fine.

lime	_____
wire	_____
dime	_____
none	_____
pint	_____
mane	_____

Name

Colour the object in each line whose name begins with 'd'.

Name

Colour in the balloons.

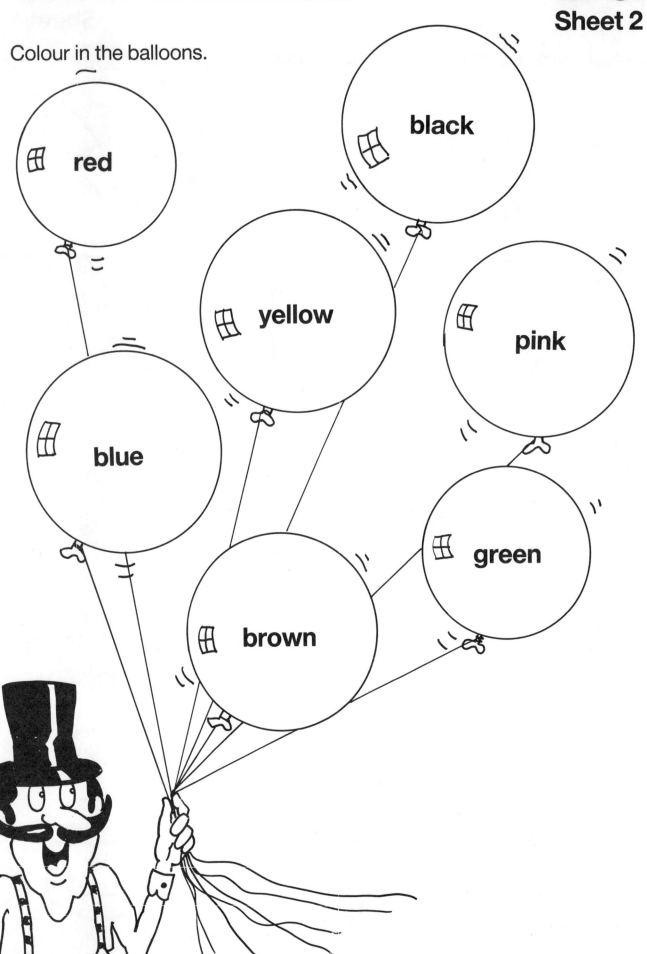

Name_____

What am I?
Write my name and draw me.

1 I have four legs.
I have soft fur.
I like to drink milk and
eat mice.
My name starts with
'c'.

I am a_____

2 I have leaves and
branches.
Birds live in me.
I give shade in
summer.
My name starts
with 't'.

I am a_____

3 People sleep in me.
I am found in a home.
I have sheets.
My name begins
with 'b'.

I am a_____

Name _____

Colour the boxes which have animal names in them.

cow	sheep	rat
fox	hat	apple
dog	kettle	pig
cat	flower	mouse

Sd

Sheet 5

Name

Look at the picture.

Colour green, the boxes of all the things you can see in the picture.

cat	table	bun	horse
tree	truck	house	cow
shark	dog	cup	sun

Name

Draw lines to match each story with its picture.

A cat caught a mouse.

A dog barked at a stranger.

The teacher read us a story.

A bird flew into a tree.

Name

seven cups

Colour each picture. Write the correct name from the list under each picture. The first one has been done for you.

six matches	two horses	seven cups
eight birds	five apples	one pencil
nine books	ten bananas	three fish

Name

Read and draw

Six cats are in a tree.

A red flower is beside a path.

Here is a big yellow balloon
and a little red balloon.

A blue car is in the shed.

Name

Rearrange the words to make a story about the picture.

man	The	fishing	the	creek
in	is	snake	crawling	its
hole	A	is	into	A
sitting	nest	a	on	bird	is

YES or NO?	
A dog can fly.	
A fish can swim.	
A boy can throw a stone.	
A ball can bounce.	
An aeroplane can skip.	
A snail has four legs.	

Name _____

Circle the correct word and draw a picture of it.

Which one is a bird?

lizard emu snake

Which one is an insect?

cup turkey ant

Which one is a fruit?

banana cow paper

Which one is a flower?

rose pen dish

Which one is a planet?

Jupiter Australia July

Name _____

Circle the correct word.

Mary (wore store) a new blue dress.

The naughty boy broke the (pillow window)

The cold (snow slow) fell on the ground.

The mouse is nibbling the (cheese bees).

Mary got a letter in the (snail mail).

We had a (coast roast) dinner on Sunday.

Name

Look at the picture.
Choose a word from the box to finish each story.
Colour the picture.

| skipping | jumping | running | bouncing |

Tony is _____ over the log.

Susan is_____ along the footpath.

Bruno is _____ the ball.

Peter is_____ over the rope.

Draw a boat on the sea.
Draw a man fishing from the boat.
Draw three birds above the boat.
Draw a sandcastle on the beach.
Draw a red and green flag on top of the sandcastle.
Draw a boy and girl beside the sandcastle.

Name _____

Write each of these words under the name headings below.

horse	sparrow	swan
grape	lemon	pear
monkey	emu	magpie
pineapple	lion	elephant

Fruit   **Animal**   **Bird**

_____   _____   _____

_____   _____   _____

_____   _____   _____

_____   _____   _____

Name _____

Code

A	B	C	D	E	F	G	H	I	J	K	L	M
⊘	□	◖	M	✳	♡	☀	🖐	♪	🐱	🐟	🥛	🥄

N	O	P	Q	R	S	T	U	V	W	X	Y	Z
🌳	✏	📖	🐑	🍎	◯	♩	🍌	☕	△	♥	←«	✉

This message has been written in code. Write the message below.

I LIKE TO EAT

ICE CREAM ON A

HOT DAY

Name

Match the lines of the nursery rhymes below.
Draw lines to connect them.

Simple Simon	went up the hill.
Little Bo Peep	sat on a tuffet.
Rub-a-dub-dub	pussy's in the well.
Jack and Jill	met a pieman.
Little Miss Muffet	runs through the town.
Little Boy Blue	sat on the wall
Ding, dong, dell,	stole a pig and away did run.
Humpty Dumpty	has lost her sheep.
Tom, Tom, the piper's son	three men in a tub.
Wee Willie Winkie	come blow your horn.

Name _____

Choose a word from the box to finish each story.

| doctor   dentist   carpenter   farmer   pilot   artist |

The _____ removed two teeth from the man.
The _____ fed the pigs with corn.
When he was sick, Mr Jones visited the _____ .
The _____ climbed into the cockpit of the large jet.
The _____ painted a picture of the sea.

Draw a picture for each story.

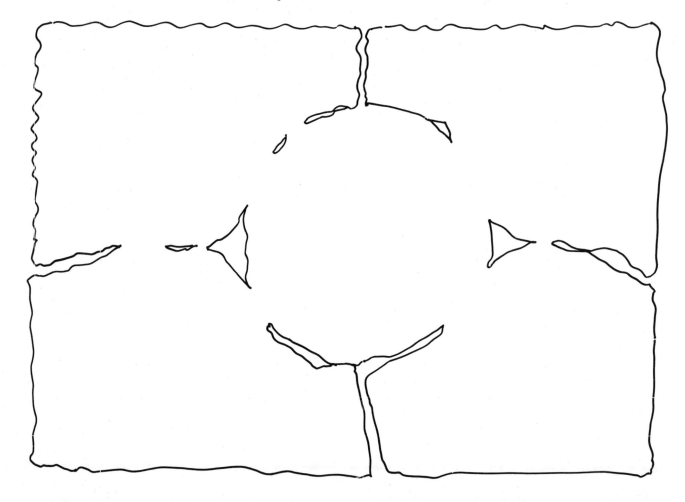

Name _____

Join the dots.

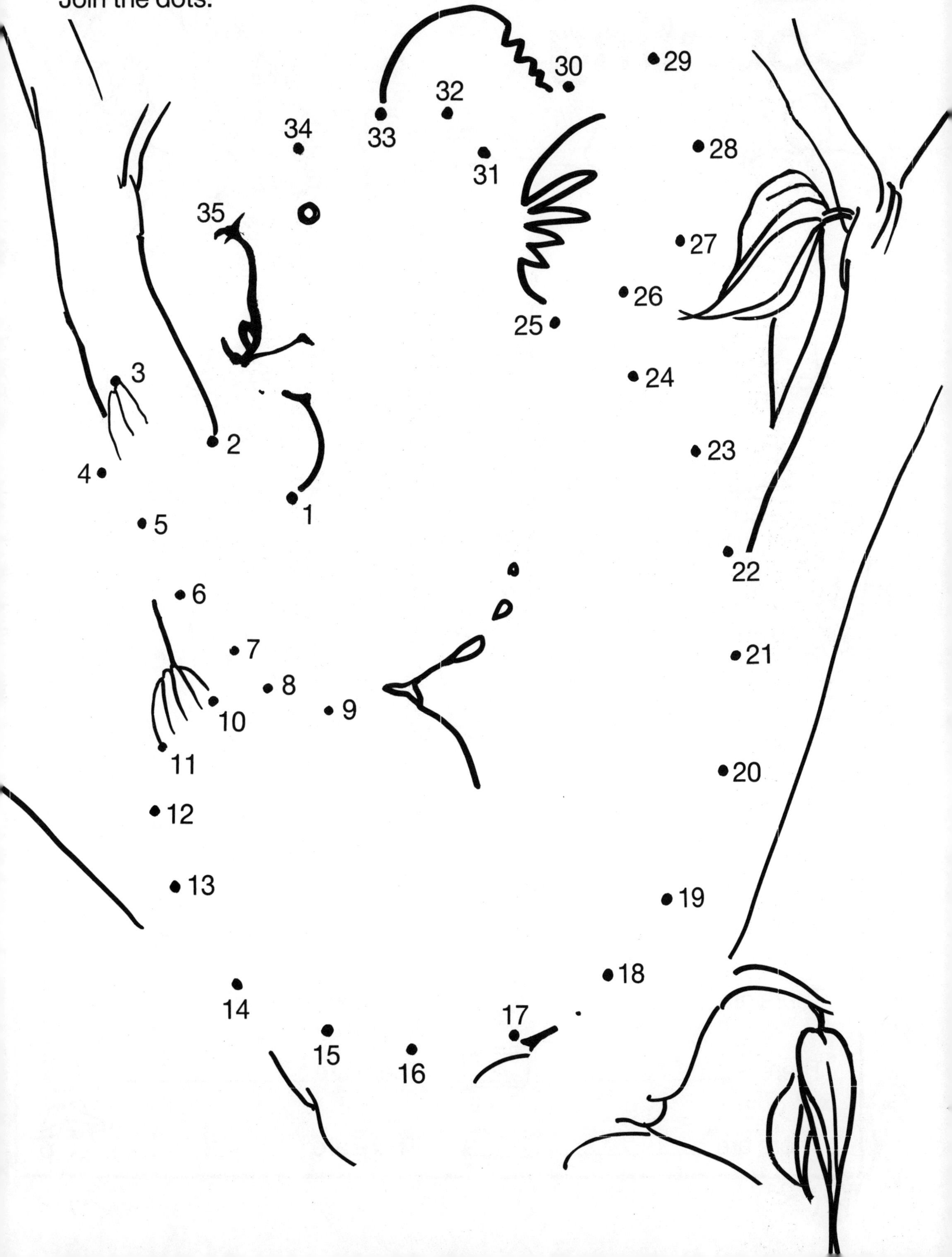

- 30
- 29
- 32
- 34
- 33
- 28
- 31
- 35
- 27
- 26
- 25
- 3
- 24
- 2
- 4
- 23
- 5
- 1
- 22
- 6
- 7
- 21
- 8
- 10
- 9
- 11
- 20
- 12
- 13
- 19
- 18
- 14
- 17
- 15
- 16

Counting

There are _____    There are _____

There are _____    There are _____

There is _____    There are _____

There are _____    There are _____

Name _____

How many are there?
Write the numeral in the box.

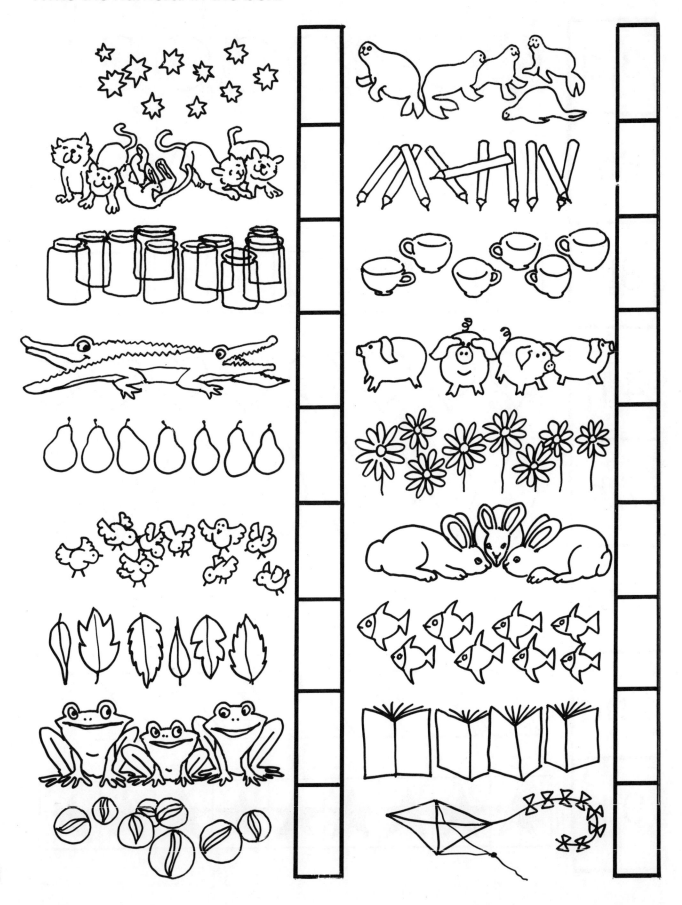

Name _____

Colour the shape in the right position.

3rd	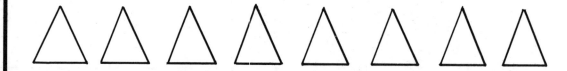
6th	
8th	
4th	
7th	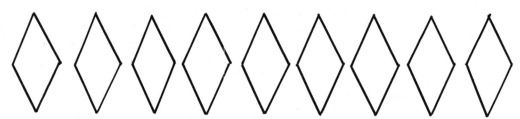
5th	
2nd	
9th	

Name

Colour the answers.

10=blue   9=green   8=red   7=yellow
6=orange   5=brown   4=black   3=purple

$1+6=$	$5+5=$	$2+6=$	$3+3=$
$3\times1=$	$10\div2=$	$6+4=$	$2\times3=$
$4+5=$	$10-3=$	$4+3=$	$7+3=$
$3\times3=$	$3+2=$	$10-4=$	$10-1=$
$2\times4=$	$2\times2=$	$2+2=$	$3+5=$
$2+3=$	$1+2=$	$8\div2=$	$6\div2=$

Name

Trace over the dotted lines to complete the second half of the picture.
Make each half a different colour.

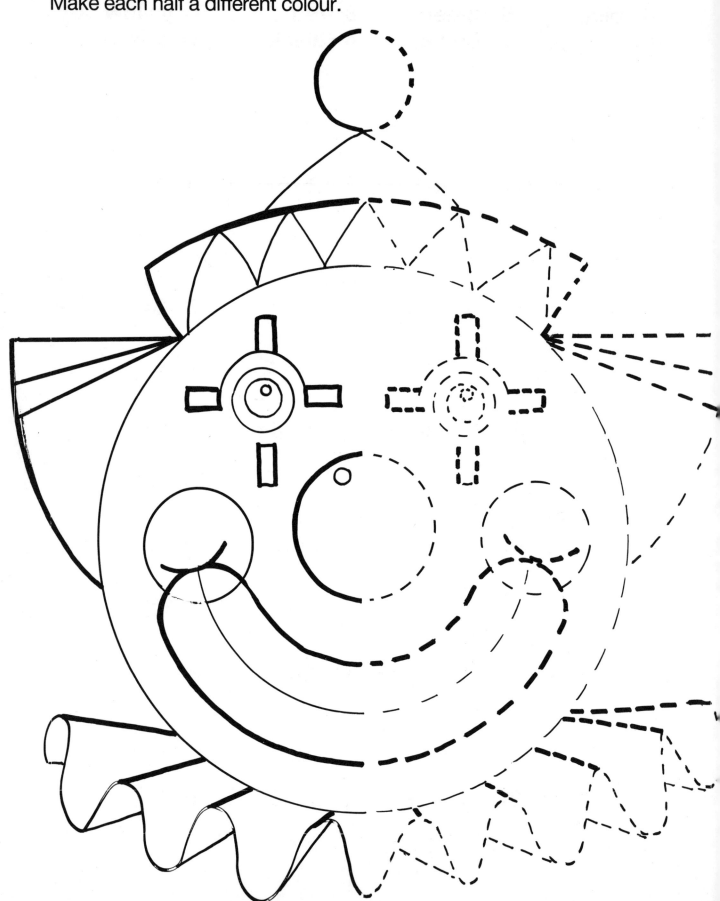

Name

Find all the triangles and colour them red.
Find all the rectangles and colour them blue.
Find all the circles and colour them black.
Find all the squares and colour them green.

Name _____

Dot-to-dot

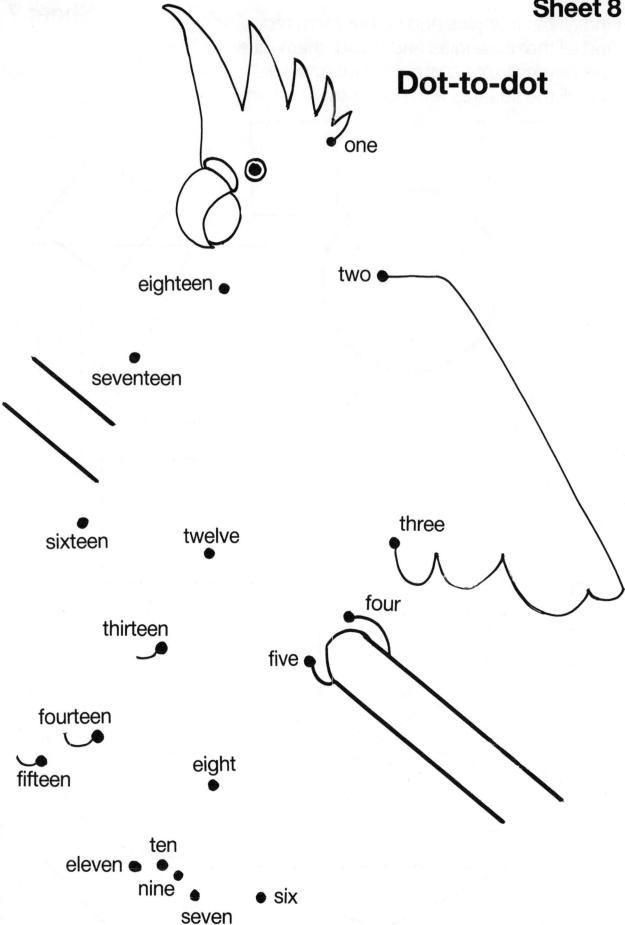

one

eighteen

two

seventeen

three

sixteen   twelve

thirteen

four

five

fourteen

fifteen

eight

ten

eleven

nine   six

seven

Name

Complete these number sentences, then colour by code.

Code

red=8
purple=11
brown=6
blue=10
yellow=15
green=12
pink=20
black=9
orange=16

$8+8=$

$5+15=$

$3\times2=$

$6+2=$

$4+4=$

$6+2=$

$2+6=$

$6+5=$

$4\times4=$

$7+5=$

$3+3=$

$6+5=$

$7+4=$

$8+8=$

$3\times5=$

$12+4=$

$1+7=$

$3+9=$

$6+6=$

$12+8=$

$6\times2=$

$10+10=$

$3\times4=$

$4\times5=$

$6+3=$

$6+5=$

$3\times3=$

$3+3=$

Name

Complete these number sentences, then colour by code.

Code

red=20
yellow=16
pink=18
brown=9
black=24

Colour the other
spaces yourself.

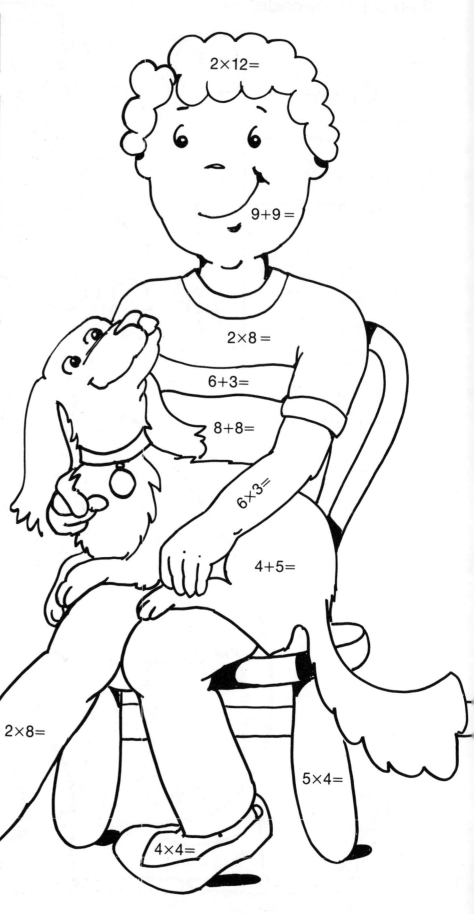

2×12=

9+9 =

2×8 =

6+3=

8+8=

6×3=

4+5=

2×8=

5×4=

4×4=

3×3=

Name _____

Pattern-making

Here is a pattern. Copy it below, then make up
patterns of your own.

Name _____

Fill in this chart to show the different eye colours in your class. Colour one eye to show each class member's eye colour.

blue	green	grey	brown
total ___	total ___	total ___	total ___

Name _____

How many number sentences can you make to equal six?
Use the numbers in the small boxes and $+$, $-$, $\times$, $\div$.

6	3	4
	1	2
5	8	9	7

_____

_____

_____

_____

_____

_____

Name

Draw the missing half of the picture.

Name

Count the squares in each row and add as many
squares as you need to give you the answer shown.
Write the numerals underneath the boxes.

eg ▢▢▢ + ▢▢▢ = 6
　　　 3 　　　 3

1 ▢▢ + ＿＿＿＿＿ = 7

2 ▢▢▢▢ + ＿＿＿＿＿ = 12

3 ▢▢▢▢ + ＿＿＿＿＿ = 14

4 ▢▢ + ＿＿＿＿＿ = 10

5 ▢▢▢ + ＿＿＿＿＿ = 9

6 ▢▢▢▢▢ + ＿＿＿＿＿ = 13

7 ▢▢▢▢▢▢ + ＿＿＿＿＿ = 11

8 ▢▢▢▢ + ＿＿＿＿＿ = 20

9 ▢▢▢▢▢▢▢▢ + ＿＿＿＿＿ = 18

Name _____

Number facts

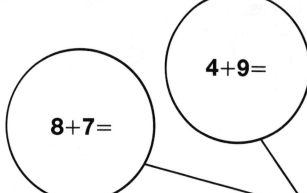

8+7=

4+9=

12+6=

7+9=

9−3=

10−7=

12−4=

15−6=

3×4=

2×9=

4×4=

5×4=

10÷2=

12÷3=

20÷5=

15÷3=

Name

Use your ruler to find which match fits in which box.
Write the number inside the box.

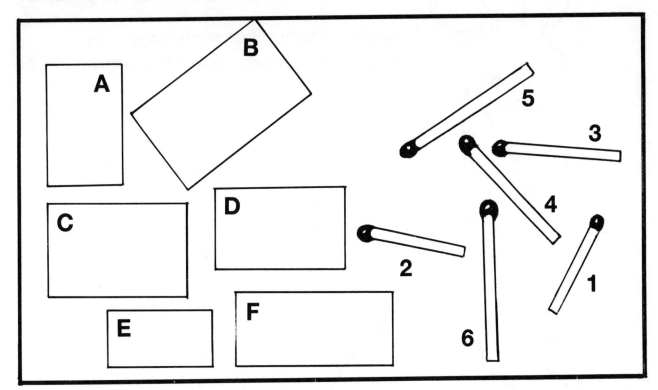

How many circles can you find?

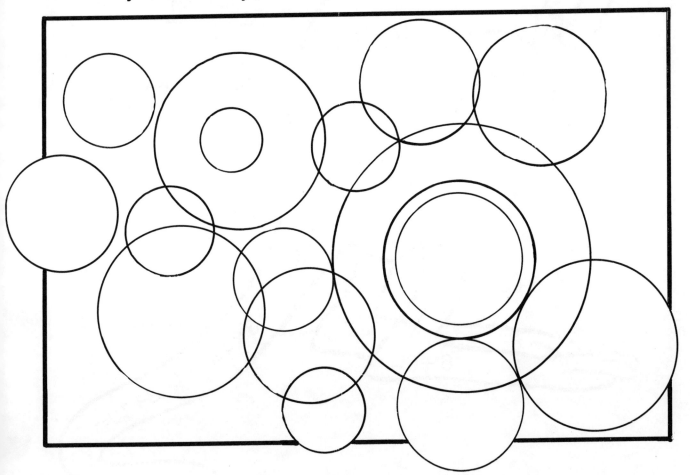

Name

Complete the number sentences.
Colour all the shapes where the answer is 12

$9+3=$

$9+3=$

$6+2=$

$7+5=$

$15-10=$

$7+5=$

$6+10=$

$2\times3=$

$7+5=$

$12\div4=$

$10+2=$

$14-2=$

$8+2=$

$8+4=$

$9+3=$

$4\times5=$

$6+4=$

$8+3=$

$2\times6=$

$4\times3=$

$10+5=$

$4+8=$

$5+8=$

$3\times4=$

$6+6=$

$2+10=$

Name _____

Look at these pictures.
Circle all those things we buy from the butcher.
Colour all those things we buy from the fruit shop.
Put a cross through all those things we buy from
the baker.

 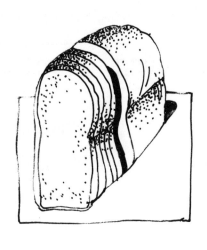 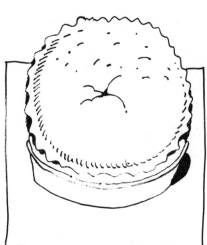

  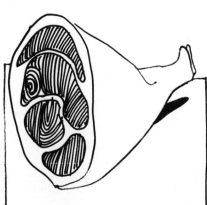

Name

Look at the picture.

Choose a word from the box to finish each story.

| feeding | collecting | milking | picking |

Michael is _____ the cows.

Penny is _____ the apples.

David is _____ the pigs.

Kate is _____ the eggs.

Draw a picture of yourself feeding some ducks.

Name

Look at the pictures.
Colour all those things we find inside a home.
Circle those things we wouldn't find inside a home.

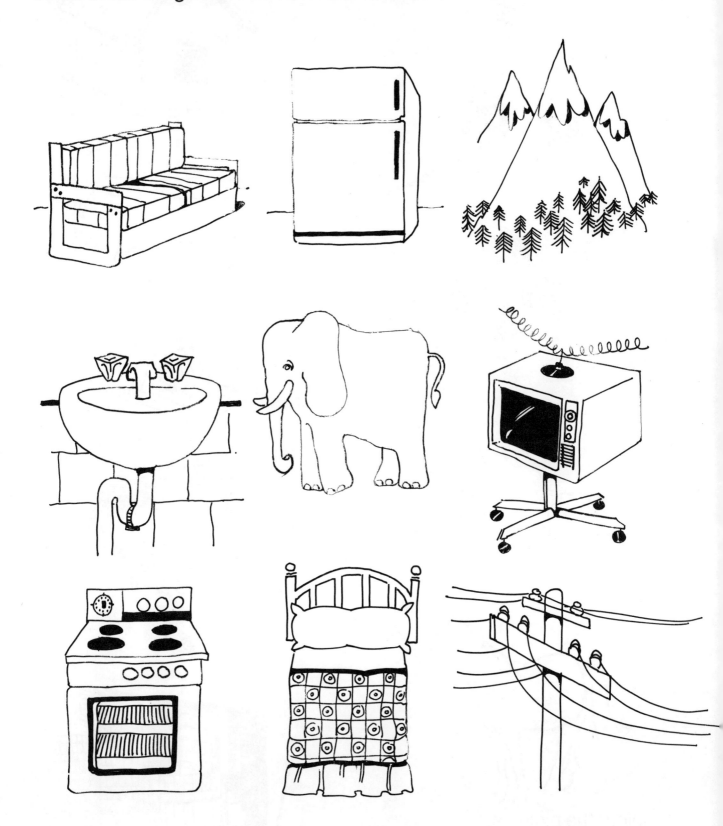

Name

Where does each animal live?
Draw a line to join each animal with its home.

Colour the pictures.

lo
Sheet 4

Name _____

Colour the animal in each row that is out of place.

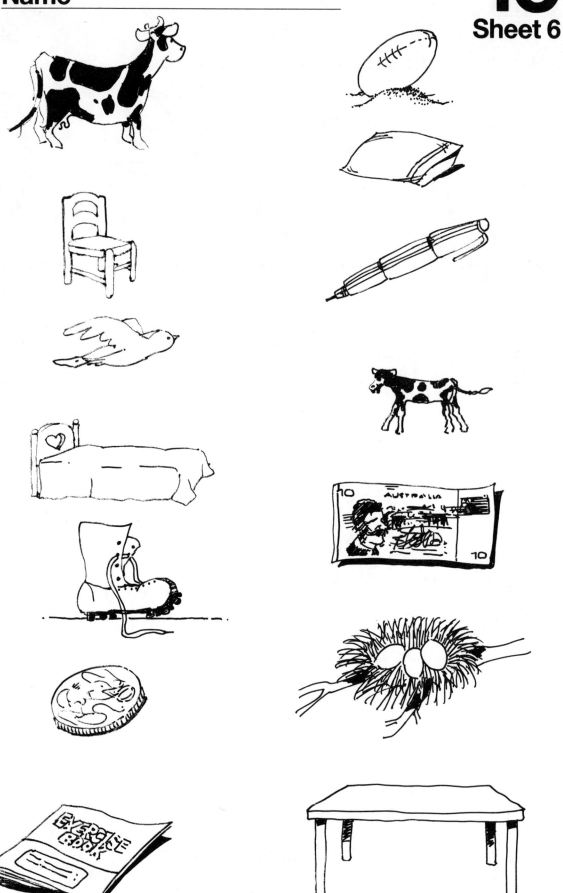

Match these things by joining them with a line.

Colour each picture.

Cut out each picture and glue it in the proper row above.

Name _____

Put a cross through the things in the picture that are unsafe.

Name

Colour the pictures below.
Cut out these pictures and rearrange them to tell a story.

Name

Look at these pictures.
Cut them out and place them under the right season.

Put a cross through the things in the picture that are dangerous.

Look at the picture. Join the words to make a true story.

Michael is   picking up papers.

Kim is   sweeping the floor.

Sally is   cleaning the blackboard.

Tony is   tidying the table.

Mimi is   watering the plants.

Look at the picture.
Choose a word from the box to finish each story.

| wood | wool | glass | rubber |

Jumpers are made of _____

Bottles are made of _____

Tyres are made of _____

Pencils are made of _____

Draw five things you need to build a house.

Name _____

Look at the picture.
Colour the thing on each shelf that is out of place.

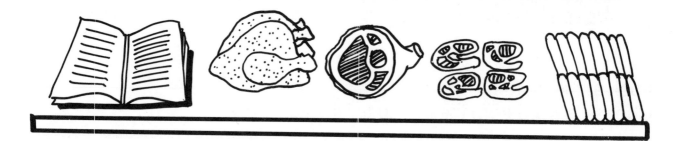

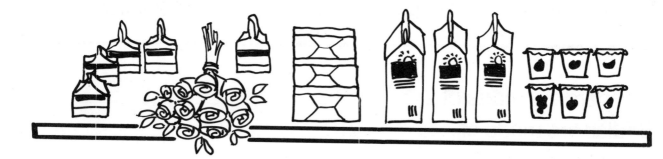

Cut out these pictures and paste them in the correct square above.
Choose a word from the box to finish each story.

| delivering | climbing | reading | stopping |

The teacher is _____ the class a story.
The policeman is _____ the traffic.
The postman is _____ a parcel.
The fireman is _____ the ladder.

Name

Look at the picture.
Draw a red line to show the way from Sally's house to Peter's house.
Draw a blue line to show the route Peter might take if he wanted to have a swim.

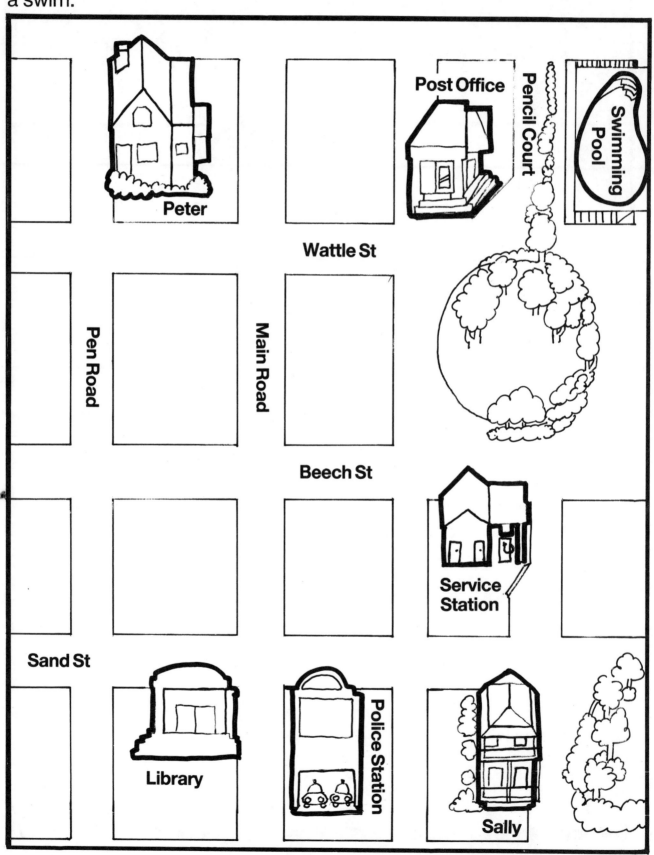

Name

Look at the picture and colour any animals
that could be pets. Draw a picture of your pet.

Look at the picture.
Choose a word from the box to finish each story.

bicycle   seven   six   hats

Tony is_____years old today.
There are_____children at his party.
Tony's present is a_____.
All the children are wearing party_____.

Find all the things in Grandma's shop that begin with 'f'.

Name

Spot the difference
Find five things in the second drawing that have been left out of the first
drawing. Colour them.

Name _____

Can you find the animal names in this word grid?
Colour each a different colour.

bear
rabbit
cow
dog
pig
tiger
ape
goat

b	c	d	p	a	g
e	o	o	i	p	o
a	w	g	g	e	a
r	a	b	b	i	t
t	i	g	e	r	x

JIM   SUE   PETER   TRISH   ADAM

Who has a cat for a pet?_____

Who has a pony for a pet?_____

Who has a puppy for a pet?_____

Who has a goldfish for a pet?_____

Who has a canary for a pet?_____

Name _____

Fruit crossword

Words   grape   pear   orange

                    apple   lemon   banana

Name

Which two things in each line are exactly the same?
Circle them.

Look at the picture.
Draw the things that are missing in the picture.

Name _____

me

Can you find
the words that rhyme?

Colour each
rhyming pair the same colour.

mouse

mean

fork

door

tie

wall

cork

fish

more

queen

flea

house

fly

ball

wish

Name

Join the pictures together to make larger words.

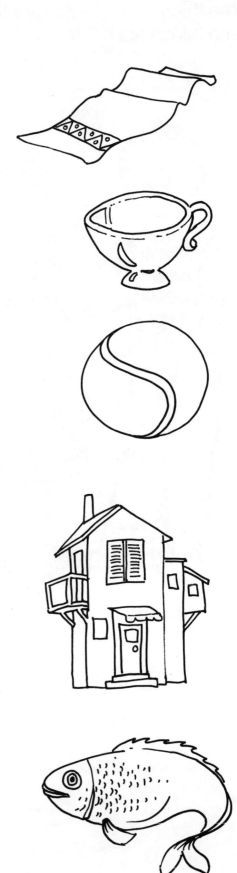

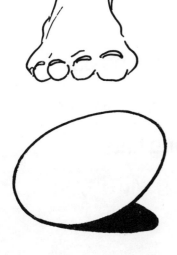

Name

Look at the four children below.
Some things about them are the same.
Some things are different.

Bruno   **Mimi**   **Rene**   **Adrian**

_____ and _____ have the same hair colour.

_____ and _____ are dressed the same way.

_____ and _____ are both wearing hats.

_____ and _____ are both playing with toys.

Name _____

Draw in the things that are missing in the picture.

Name

Colour all the things in the picture that begin with 't'.

Name

Look at the two pictures carefully.
In the second picture put an X through the things that are different.

Name

All of these animals have something missing. Can you draw the missing parts?

Name _____

Can you help the bird find a path to its nest?

Name

Words
house   cup   tent

Complete the crossword.

Words
tree   horse
train   ship

Name

Use the first letter of each word in the picture
to find the name of a mystery object. Write the word and draw the object.

Join the things that go together, with a line.

Colour each pair
a different colour.